Splenda ®
No Calorie Sweetener

pil

Publications International, Ltd.
Favorite Brand Name Recipes at www.fbnr.com

Nutritional Analysis: Every effort has been made to check the accuracy of the nutritional analyses in this book. However, because numerous variables account for a wide range of values for certain foods, nutritive analyses in this book should be considered approximate.

Microwave Cooking: Microwave ovens vary in wattage. Use the cooking times as guidelines and check for doneness before adding more time.

Contents

38

67

75

76

Splenda®
No Calorie Sweetener

Now you can indulge your sweet cravings. This collection brings you great tasting recipes with fewer calories than full-sugar counterparts. So when you yearn for something sweet, go ahead—indulge yourself. You can have sweetness without all the calories and carbohydrates of sugar.

SPLENDA® No Calorie Sweetener is made from sugar, so it tastes like sugar. It is available in two forms: Granular, which measures and pours like sugar, and Packets, individual portions to add to beverages or food.

SPLENDA® No Calorie Sweetener contains the ingredient sucralose. Sucralose is made from sugar; however, the body does not process it as a sugar or a carbohydrate so it doesn't affect blood glucose levels, making it suitable for people with diabetes. Like most other no calorie sweeteners, a serving of SPLENDA® No Calorie Sweetener contains a small amount of the common food ingredients, dextrose and/or maltodextrin, for volume. These contribute less than 1g carbohydrate and less than 5 calories per serving to SPLENDA® No Calorie Sweetener, and meet the FDA definition of no-calorie foods.

SPLENDA® Granular is formulated specifically so it measures, pours and sweetens like sugar. SPLENDA®

Granular also stays sweet with heat, so it can also be used in cooking and baking!

COOKING AND BAKING WITH SPLENDA® GRANULAR

SPLENDA® Granular can be used almost anywhere you use sugar in cooking and baking.

Replacing sugar for sweetness

SPLENDA® Granular works best in recipes to replace sugar's sweetness, such as in pie fillings, cheesecakes, sweet sauces, marinades and glazes. SPLENDA® Granular also works well in quick breads, muffins and cookies.

Replacing sugar when sugar does more than sweeten

In some recipes, sugar and other caloric sweeteners, such as honey, brown sugar, molasses and maple syrup, provide not just sweetness, but other important characteristics:

• Sugars can give structure, texture and volume.

• Sugars may enhance caramelization and browning.
• Sugars can help retain moistness and tenderness in baked goods.
• Sugars can act as preservatives, keeping baked goods fresh.

In recipes where sugar is providing more than sweetness, it is helpful to understand a few tips for cooking and baking with SPLENDA® Granular.

PROPORTIONS AND VOLUME

Baked goods: Since sugar contributes volume to many recipes, you may notice a smaller yield in your recipe when substituting SPLENDA® Granular for sugar. Some cakes and cookies will not rise as high as their full-sugar counterparts. However, they will still taste delicious. The recipes in this cookbook have been developed to achieve volume. When adapting your own recipes, try adding ½ cup nonfat dry milk powder and ½ teaspoon of baking soda for every 1 cup of SPLENDA® Granular to maintain volume.

Confections: Should you desire to adapt your own confection recipes, you may wish to replace only a portion of the sugar. In recipes where the amount of sugar is quite high, such as caramel, pecan pies, and angel food or pound cakes, complete substitution of SPLENDA® Granular for all the sweeteners may not yield the best results. A blend of sugar with SPLENDA® No Calorie Sweetener is recommended instead of full sugar replacement.

BROWNING

There are several ways you can obtain that familiar golden brown color when baking with SPLENDA® Granular. Try one of the following:
• Add 1 to 2 tablespoons molasses to your recipe.
• Remove your baked goods 4 to 5 minutes before the end of the baking time, brush the crust or tops with 1 to 2 tablespoons beaten egg white, milk, honey or maple syrup. Or, spray the crust or tops lightly with nonstick cooking spray. Return to the hot oven for 4 to 5 minutes or until the top browns lightly.

STORAGE

Sugar acts as a preservative, helps retain moisture and keeps baked goods fresher longer.

Baked goods made with SPLENDA® Granular will stay fresh for 24 hours when stored in an airtight container at room temperature. For longer storage, freeze them in an airtight container.

In canning jams and jellies, SPLENDA® Granular does not provide preserving properties. Consult a sugarless canning cookbook or www.splenda.com for best directions for incorporating SPLENDA® Granular in jams and jellies.

For additional recipes and to learn more about cooking and baking with SPLENDA® Granular, please visit our website at www. splenda.com.

Sweet Starts

Delicious ways to begin the day

Golden Pumpkin Loaf

Prep time: *15 minutes*
Bake time: *40 to 45 minutes*

⅓	cup plain nonfat yogurt
1	tablespoon nonfat sour cream
2	cups pumpkin purée
3	eggs
¼	cup vegetable oil
2½	cups all-purpose flour
¾	cup SPLENDA® Granular
1	tablespoon plus 1 teaspoon baking powder
1	tablespoon pumpkin pie spice
1	cup raisins
¼	cup chopped walnuts

PREHEAT oven to 350°F. Spray 2 (9×5-inch) loaf pans with nonstick cooking spray.

BLEND yogurt, sour cream, pumpkin, eggs and vegetable oil in large bowl. Add flour, SPLENDA® Granular, baking powder and pumpkin pie spice.

STIR, scraping sides of bowl, and mix in raisins and walnuts.

SPREAD batter into prepared pans. Bake 45 to 50 minutes or until toothpick inserted in center comes out clean.

COOL and cut each loaf into 8 slices.

Makes 16 slices

Nutrients per serving
Serving size: 1 slice
Total calories: 180
Calories from fat: 50
Total fat: 6g
Saturated fat: 1g
Cholesterol: 40mg
Sodium: 140mg
Total carbohydrate: 28g
Dietary fiber: 2g
Sugars: 8g
Protein: 5g
Exchanges per serving
2 Starch, 1 Fat

Cinnamon Swirl Coffeecake

Prep time: *20 minutes*
Bake time: *50 to 60 minutes*

3	cups cake flour
1	tablespoon baking powder
¾	teaspoon baking soda
½	cup unsalted butter, softened
1⅓	cups SPLENDA® Granular
1	egg
¼	cup egg substitute
2	teaspoons vanilla extract
½	cup unsweetened applesauce
1½	cups reduced fat sour cream
3	tablespoons brown sugar
2	tablespoons ground cinnamon

PREHEAT oven to 350°F. Spray 10-inch tube pan or nonstick Bundt pan with cooking oil spray.

SIFT cake flour, baking powder, and soda into medium bowl. In large bowl, cream softened butter with electric mixer on medium speed. Add SPLENDA® Granular and egg. Mix until smooth. Add egg substitute and vanilla; mix 30 seconds. Add applesauce and ½ cup sour cream; mix until smooth. Add sifted flour mixture and beat at medium speed just until smooth. Add remaining sour cream and blend. Set aside.

MAKE spiced filling: Place 1 cup cake batter in a small bowl. Add brown sugar and cinnamon; blend.

PLACE ½ remaining cake batter into prepared pan. Top with spiced batter filling. Swirl with knife. Top with remaining batter.

BAKE 50 to 60 minutes or until toothpick inserted in center comes out clean.

Makes 16 slices

Nutrients per serving
Serving size: 1 slice (¹⁄₁₆ cake)
Total calories: 200
Calories from fat: 70
Total fat: 8g
Saturated fat: 5g
Cholesterol: 25mg
Sodium: 180mg
Total carbohydrate: 28g
Dietary fiber: 1g
Sugars: 5g
Protein: 4g
Exchanges per serving
2 Starch, 1 Fat

Dried Cherry and Almond Scones

Prep time: *15 minutes*
Bake time: *10 to 15 minutes*

- 1   egg
- 1   egg white
- ⅓   cup canola oil
- ⅔   cup SPLENDA® Granular
- ½   cup buttermilk
- ½   teaspoon almond extract
- ⅓   cup nonfat instant dry milk
- 1   teaspoon baking powder
- ½   teaspoon baking soda
- 2   cups all-purpose flour
- 1   cup dried cherries, chopped
- 2   tablespoons sugar (optional)

PREHEAT oven to 350°F. Spray cookie sheet or jelly roll pan with nonstick cooking spray.

BLEND egg and egg white in large mixing bowl. Add canola oil, SPLENDA® Granular, buttermilk, almond extract and nonfat dry milk; stir. Mix baking powder, baking soda and flour. Blend into buttermilk mixture. Add dried cherries and stir. Mound 12 spoonfuls of batter on prepared baking sheet. Lightly sprinkle scones with sugar, if desired.

BAKE 10 to 15 minutes. Serve warm. Scones may be frozen and reheated.

Makes 12 servings

Nutrients per serving
Serving size: 1 scone
Total calories: 190
Calories from fat: 60
Total fat: 7g
Saturated fat: 0.5g
Cholesterol: 20mg
Sodium: 125mg
Total carbohydrate: 27g
Dietary fiber: 2g
Sugars: 8g
Protein: 4g
Exchanges per serving
2 Starch, 1 Fat

French Toast Strata

Prep time: Make ahead
Bake time: 40 to 50 minutes

- ⅓ cup SPLENDA® Granular
- 1 cup egg substitute
- ⅔ cup skim milk
- 1 teaspoon vanilla extract
- ¾ teaspoon maple extract
- 8 slices cinnamon raisin bread
- 2 cups apples, peeled, cored and thinly sliced
- ¼ cup low-fat cream cheese
- 1 tablespoon SPLENDA® Granular
- ½ teaspoon ground cinnamon

PREHEAT oven to 350°F. Spray 8×8-inch square pan with nonstick cooking spray.

BLEND ⅓ cup SPLENDA® Granular, egg substitute, milk and vanilla and maple extracts in medium bowl.

TEAR cinnamon raisin bread into small pieces (1×2 inches). Toss bread and sliced apples with egg mixture in bowl. Coat bread evenly and pour into prepared pan.

CUT cream cheese into 8 chunks and place on top. Blend remaining 1 tablespoon SPLENDA® Granular and cinnamon together. Sprinkle over strata. Cover and refrigerate overnight.

BAKE 40 to 50 minutes or until lightly browned and set. Serve immediately.

Makes 8 servings

Nutrients per serving
Serving size: 2×4-inch slice
Total calories: 130
Calories from fat: 25
Total fat: 2.5g
Saturated fat: 1g
Cholesterol: . . . .<5mg
Sodium: 200mg
Total carbohydrate: 20g
Dietary fiber: 2g
Sugars: 5g
Protein: 7g
Exchanges per serving
½ Fat, 1½ Starch, ½ Fruit

Lemon Poppyseed Muffins

Prep time: 20 minutes
Bake time: 12 to 15 minutes

2¼ cups cake flour
¾ cup SPLENDA® Granular
¼ cup sugar
¾ cup unsalted butter, softened
½ cup nonfat instant dry milk
2 teaspoons baking powder
¾ teaspoon baking soda
¼ teaspoon salt
¾ cup buttermilk
2 tablespoons fresh lemon juice
2½ tablespoons grated lemon peel
3 eggs
2 teaspoons vanilla extract
2 tablespoons poppyseeds

Nutrients per serving	
Serving size: 1 muffin	
Total calories:	170
Calories from fat:	80
Total fat:	9g
Saturated fat:	5g
Cholesterol:	55mg
Sodium:	170mg
Total carbohydrate:	17g
Dietary fiber:	0g
Sugars:	5g
Protein:	4g
Exchanges per serving	
1½ Starch, 2 Fat	

PREHEAT oven to 350°F. Place
18 paper baking cups in muffin pans. Set aside.

PLACE cake flour, SPLENDA® Granular, sugar and softened unsalted
butter in large mixing bowl. Mix on medium speed 1 to 2 minutes
with an electric mixer until blended and crumbly.

ADD nonfat dry milk, baking powder, baking soda and salt. Mix on
low speed until blended.

BLEND buttermilk, lemon juice, lemon zest and peel, eggs and vanilla
in small bowl. Add ⅔ of buttermilk mixture to flour mixture. Mix on
medium speed 1 minute. Stop and scrape sides and bottom of bowl.
Mix on medium-high speed 45 to 60 seconds. Reduce mixer speed to
low and add remaining liquid; blend. Stop mixer and scrape sides and
bottom of bowl again. Add poppyseeds. Mix on medium-high speed
30 seconds.

POUR muffin batter into prepared pans. Bake muffins 12 to 15 minutes
or until toothpick inserted in center comes out clean.

Makes 18 muffins

Low-Fat Bran Muffins

Prep time: *10 minutes*
Bake Time: *20 to 25 minutes*

¼	cup unsweetened applesauce
1	egg
1½	cups low-fat buttermilk
3	tablespoons canola oil
2	teaspoons vanilla extract
⅛	teaspoon salt
¼	cup nonfat instant dry milk
¾	cup SPLENDA® Granular
1	cup wheat bran, divided
1½	cups all-purpose flour
1½	teaspoons baking soda
1	teaspoon ground cinnamon
2	tablespoons flaxseeds
2	tablespoons dried currants or raisins

PREHEAT oven to 350°F. Oil or line muffin pans with paper baking cups.

BLEND applesauce, egg, buttermilk, oil, vanilla, salt, nonfat dry milk and SPLENDA® Granular together in large mixing bowl, using wire whisk. Reserve 2 tablespoons wheat bran for topping. Add remaining wheat bran, flour, baking soda and cinnamon to applesauce mixture; stir well. Mix in flaxseeds and currants.

FILL muffin cups with batter. Top each cup with sprinkle of wheat bran flakes. Bake 20 to 25 minutes or until toothpick inserted in center comes out clean.

Makes 12 muffins

Nutrients per serving
Serving size: 1 muffin

Total calories:	150
Calories from fat:	45
Total fat:	5g
Saturated fat:	0.5g
Cholesterol:	20mg
Sodium:	135mg
Total carbohydrate:	21g
Dietary fiber:	3g
Sugars:	4g
Protein:	5g

Exchanges per serving
1½ Starch, 1 Fat

Blueberry Corn Muffins

Prep time: 10 minutes
Bake time: 20 to 25 minutes

1¾	cups all-purpose flour
½	cup yellow cornmeal
1¼	teaspoons baking powder
½	teaspoon baking soda
½	teaspoon salt
¾	cup SPLENDA® Granular
½	cup unsalted butter, softened
⅓	cup egg substitute
2	teaspoons vanilla extract
1	cup buttermilk
1	cup blueberries (frozen or fresh)

PREHEAT oven to 350°F. Spray muffin pan with nonstick cooking spray or line muffin pans with 10 paper baking cups.

BLEND dry ingredients together in medium mixing bowl. Set aside.

BLEND butter in mixing bowl until light and fluffy. Add egg substitute slowly. Scrape sides and continue to mix until butter forms small lumps. Add vanilla and buttermilk. Mix well. Add dry ingredients in 3 batches. Mix well and scrape sides of bowl after each addition.

FOLD blueberries gently into batter. Scoop batter into prepared muffin cups, filling cups to top. Bake 20 to 25 minutes or until toothpick inserted in center comes out clean.

Makes 10 muffins

Nutrients per serving
Serving size: 1 muffin
Total calories 220
Calories from fat 90
Total fat 10g
Saturated fat 6g
Cholesterol 25mg
Sodium 290mg
Total carbohydrate 26g
Dietary fiber 2g
Sugars 3g
Protein 5g
Exchanges Per Serving
1½ Starch, 2 Fat

Light
Lunches

Go light for mid-day breaks

Cucumber and Onion Salad

Prep time: 15 minutes
Chill time: 2 hours

2½ cups thinly sliced, unpeeled cucumbers (sliced lengthwise)
½ cup peeled and thinly sliced red onion
⅓ cup SPLENDA® Granular
⅓ cup white vinegar
¼ teaspoon salt
⅛ teaspoon black pepper

TOSS cucumbers and onions together in medium, nonreactive bowl. Set aside.

WHISK together remaining ingredients in separate bowl until blended. Pour over cucumbers and onions. Cover and chill 2 hours; stir several times.

NOTE: To quickly slice cucumbers lengthwise, use a mandoline. Or you may slice them into thin disks.

Makes 6 servings (¾ cup)

Nutrients per serving
Serving size: ¾ cup
Total calories: 15
Calories from fat: 0
Total fat: 0g
Saturated fat: 0g
Cholesterol: 0mg
Sodium: 100mg
Total carbohydrate: 3g
Dietary fiber: 0g
Sugars: 2g
Protein: 0g
Exchanges per serving
Free

Sweet and Spicy BLT

Prep time: *10 minutes*

Seasoning Mix
- 1 tablespoon SPLENDA® Granular
- ¼ teaspoon ground cayenne pepper
- ¼ teaspoon garlic powder
- 1 teaspoon paprika

COMBINE all ingredients in small bowl and mix well. Store in an airtight container or storage bag until ready to use.

Makes about 4 servings (1 teaspoon)

Sandwich
- 2 slices extra lean turkey bacon
- 1 teaspoon Seasoning Mix (see above)
- 2 slices wheat bread
- 1 tablespoon fat-free ranch salad dressing
- 1 leaf green lettuce
- 2 slices fresh tomato

Nutrients per serving
Serving size: 1 sandwich

Total calories:	230
Calories from fat:	66
Total fat:	7g
Saturated fat:	1g
Cholesterol:	20mg
Sodium:	820mg
Total carbohydrate:	31g
Dietary fiber:	3g
Sugars:	4g
Protein:	9g

Exchanges per serving
2 Starch, 1 Meat, 1 Fat

PLACE bacon on microwave-safe pan. Top each slice with ½ teaspoon seasoning mix. Cook bacon in microwave according to package directions.

TOAST bread, then spread with ranch dressing. Layer cooked bacon, lettuce and tomato slices on bread to make sandwich. Serve immediately.

Makes 1 sandwich

Raw Broccoli Salad

Prep Time: 5 to 10 minutes

4 cups (about 2 pounds) broccoli florets or broccolini
¼ cup minced red onion
2 tablespoons SPLENDA® Granular
2 tablespoons cider vinegar
2 tablespoons low-fat mayonnaise

Raw Broccoli Salad, continued

2 tablespoons sunflower seeds
     shelled, roasted and salted
3 tablespoons seedless raisins

CHOP broccoli or broccolini into florets. Set aside.

WHISK together remaining ingredients in medium bowl. Add broccoli. Toss to coat. Chill until ready to serve.

Makes 6 servings (²⁄₃ cup)

Nutrients per serving	
Serving size: ²⁄₃ cup	
Total calories:	60
Calories from fat:	30
Total fat:	2g
Saturated fat:	0g
Cholesterol:	0mg
Sodium:	60mg
Total carbohydrate:	9g
Dietary fiber:	1g
Sugars:	5g
Protein:	2g
Exchanges per serving	
2 Vegetable	

Creamy Cole Slaw

Prep time: 20 minutes
Chill time: 2 hours

1½ cups low-fat mayonnaise
 ⅓ cup SPLENDA® Granular
 3 tablespoons finely chopped
     sweet onion
 2 teaspoons lemon juice
 1 tablespoon white wine vinegar
 ¼ teaspoon celery seed
 ¾ teaspoon salt
 ¼ teaspoon black pepper
 1 bag (8 cups) prepared shredded cabbage cole slaw mix
 ½ cup shredded carrots

BLEND mayonnaise, SPLENDA® Granular, onion, lemon juice, vinegar, celery seed, salt and pepper in large bowl.

ADD cole slaw mix and carrots. Stir well.

CHILL two hours. Stir again just before serving.

Makes 10 servings (¾ cup)

Nutrients per serving	
Serving size: ¾ cup	
Total calories:	80
Calories from fat:	20
Total fat:	2g
Saturated fat:	0g
Cholesterol:	5mg
Sodium:	520mg
Total carbohydrate:	15g
Dietary fiber:	2g
Sugars:	6g
Protein:	1g
Exchanges per serving	
½ Starch, 1 Vegetable	

Orange-Almond Salad

Prep time: *15 minutes*

3 cups assorted salad greens
2 navel oranges, peeled and separated into sections
½ cup thinly sliced celery
2 tablespoons chopped green onion
¼ cup cider vinegar
¼ cup SPLENDA® Granular
2 teaspoons vegetable oil
¼ cup toasted slivered almonds

COMBINE greens, orange sections, celery, and green onion in large bowl. Set aside.

BLEND vinegar, SPLENDA® Granular and vegetable oil in small bowl. Whisk until smooth. Drizzle dressing mixture evenly over greens mixture. Toss gently to coat.

PORTION salad evenly among 4 plates, about 1¼ cups per plate. Sprinkle 1 scant tablespoon slivered almonds over each serving. Serve immediately.

Makes 4 servings (1¼ cups)

Nutrients per serving
Serving size: 1¼ cups
Total calories: 120
Calories from fat: 60
Total fat: 6g
Saturated fat: 0g
Cholesterol: 0mg
Sodium: 25mg
Total carbohydrate: 16g
Dietary fiber: 5g
Sugars: 7g
Protein: 3g
Exchanges per serving
½ Fruit, 1 Vegetable, 1 Fat

Chili Vegetarian Style

Prep time: *20 minutes*
Cook time: *30 minutes*

1   tablespoon extra-virgin olive oil
1   jalapeño pepper,* seeded and finely chopped
½   cup chopped onion
1⅓ cups diced red and yellow bell peppers
6   teaspoons chili powder
1½ teaspoons paprika
¼   teaspoon garlic powder
¾   teaspoon ground red pepper
⅓   cup SPLENDA® Granular
3   tablespoons cider vinegar
1   can (28 ounces) crushed tomatoes
2   cans (15 ounces each) black beans, undrained
2   cans (15 ounces each) dark red kidney beans, undrained
1   can (15 ounces) cannellini or other beans, undrained
1   box (10 ounces) frozen corn kernels
    Salt

Jalepeño peppers can sting and irritate the skin. Wear rubber gloves when handling peppers and do not touch the eyes.

HEAT olive oil in large stock pot. Sauté jalapeño, onion and bell peppers over medium heat until onions are translucent, about 5 to 8 minutes.

ADD remaining ingredients, and season to taste with salt. Bring to boil, cover and simmer over low heat for 20 minutes. Serve hot.*

Makes 16 servings (1 cup)

***NOTE:** Make ahead for best flavor. For spicy chili, increase ground red pepper to 1 teaspoon and increase chili powder to 7 teaspoons.

If sweeter taste is preferred, increase SPLENDA® Granular to ⅔ cup.

Nutrients per serving	
Serving size: 1 cup	
Total calories:	150
Calories from fat:	20
Total fat:	2g
Saturated fat:	0g
Cholesterol:	0mg
Sodium:	590mg
Total carbohydrate:	27g
Dietary fiber:	9g
Sugars:	4g
Protein:	8g
Exchanges per serving	
1 Starch, 3 Vegetable	

Warm Spinach Salad

Prep time: 15 minutes

1	bag (7 ounces) baby spinach greens
½	cup nonfat salad croutons
¼	cup white vinegar
¼	cup water
¼	cup Dijon mustard
3	tablespoons SPLENDA® Granular
5	slices turkey bacon
¼	cup chopped red onion
2	cloves garlic, peeled and minced

PLACE spinach greens in colander. Wash and remove stems; drain well. Place in serving bowl and add croutons.

BLEND vinegar, water, mustard and SPLENDA® Granular. Set aside.

SLICE bacon into small, thin strips. Place in medium saucepan and fry over medium-high heat until crispy, about 3 to 4 minutes.

ADD onion and garlic and cook over medium-high heat 1 to 2 minutes, stirring often.

ADD vinegar mixture and simmer 1 to 2 minutes. Pour over spinach and croutons. Toss well. Serve immediately.

Makes 4 servings (1¾ cups)

Nutrients per serving
Serving size: 1¾ cups
Total calories: 90
Calories from fat: 30
Total fat: 3.5g
Saturated fat: 1g
Cholesterol: 10mg
Sodium: 660mg
Total carbohydrate: 5g
Dietary fiber: 5g
Sugars: 1g
Protein: 5g
Exchanges per serving
1 Fat, 1 Vegetable

Curried Turkey and Apple Salad

Prep time: *20 minutes*

  1 tablespoon canola oil
  1 tablespoon curry powder
  ¼ cup diced onion
  2 tablespoons fresh lemon juice
  2 tablespoons SPLENDA® Granular
  ¼ teaspoon salt (optional)
  ½ cup low-fat mayonnaise
  2 stalks celery, thinly sliced
  1 pound roasted turkey breast, cut into ½-inch dice
  1 medium apple, cut into ¼-inch dice
     Salad greens
  ⅓ cup chopped dried apricots, for garnish

HEAT oil in small saucepan over medium-high heat. Add curry powder and onion. Cook and stir 1 to 2 minutes or until onions are tender. Add lemon juice, SPLENDA® Granular and salt. Simmer over medium heat until sauce begins to thicken, about 1 minute. Remove from heat and cool.

STIR mayonnaise into cooled sauce; mix well. Toss together celery, turkey and apple in large bowl. Add dressing and gently toss until evenly coated.

SERVE turkey mixture mounded on salad greens, garnished with chopped apricots, if desired.

Makes 4 servings (¾ cup)

Nutrients per serving
Serving size: ¾ cup
Total calories: 300
Calories from fat: 60
Total fat: 6g
Saturated fat: 0.5g
Cholesterol: 100mg
Sodium: 360mg
Total carbohydrate: 24g
Dietary fiber: 3g
Sugars: 12g
Protein: 35g
Exchanges per serving
1 Starch, ½ Fruit, 4 Meat

Daily
Dinners

Easy enough for weeknights, delicious enough for parties!

Quick Glazed Pork Loin

Prep time: 10 minutes
Bake time: 25 to 30 minutes

1 (1 to 1½-pound) pork tenderloin
¼ cup water
2 tablespoons tomato paste
1 tablespoon orange juice concentrate
2½ teaspoons chili powder
⅛ teaspoon salt
1 tablespoon SPLENDA® Granular
1 teaspoon white vinegar
1 package (14 ounces) frozen mixed vegetables

PREHEAT oven to 425°F. Rinse pork loin and pat dry. Set aside.

MIX water, tomato paste, orange juice concentrate, chili powder, salt, SPLENDA® Granular and white vinegar, in small bowl. Whisk until smooth.

PLACE pork loin in foil-lined 13×9-inch baking pan. Cover with half of glaze. Bake 15 minutes.

REMOVE pork loin from oven. Cover with remaining glaze. Place vegetables around pork loin. Bake an additional 15 minutes or until vegetables are hot and pork loin internal temperature reaches 160°F.

Makes 4 servings

Nutrients per serving
Serving size: 3 ounces pork and ½ cup vegetables
Total calories: 180
Calories from fat: 36
Total fat: 4g
Saturated fat: 1.5g
Cholesterol: 75mg
Sodium: 220mg
Total carbohydrate: 9g
Dietary fiber: 3g
Sugars: 3g
Protein: 29g
Exchanges per serving
½ Starch, 3 Meat, 1 Vegetable

Baked Salmon with Orange-Ginger Sauce

Prep time: 15 minutes
Bake time: 10 to 15 minutes

1   (2½-inch) section fresh gingerroot
1   cup orange juice
¼   cup SPLENDA® Granular
2   tablespoons nonfat half-and-half
¼   teaspoon cornstarch
¼   teaspoon salt
2   tablespoons unsalted butter, softened
2   cups frozen stir-fry vegetables
2   salmon fillets (10 ounces raw, weight will reduce after baking)

PREHEAT oven to 450°F.

MAKE sauce: Peel gingerroot and slice into 10 slices. Pour orange juice into small saucepan. Add SPLENDA® Granular and gingerroot. Bring to rolling boil over medium-high heat. Boil 10 to 12 minutes or until reduced to 2 to 3 tablespoons. Remove from heat and lift out gingerroot with fork. Set aside.

MIX half-and-half, cornstarch and salt. Whisk softened butter, 1 tablespoon at a time, into orange juice mixture. Stir until melted. Add half-and-half mixture to saucepan. Stir well. Place saucepan back on heat. Bring to simmer over medium-high heat.

REMOVE sauce from heat and mix in blender 15 to 20 seconds or until smooth and light in color. Set aside.

PREPARE salmon: Place vegetables in oiled 8×8-inch baking pan. Place salmon fillets on vegetables. Bake 10 to 15 minutes or until fully cooked and tender. Place vegetables and salmon on serving plates. Spoon sauce over salmon. Serve with steamed rice, if desired.

Makes 2 servings
(4 ounces salmon and 1 cup vegetables)

Nutrients per serving
Serving size: 4 ounces salmon and 1 cup vegetables
Total calories: 490
Calories from fat: 230
Total fat: 27g
Saturated fat: 10g
Cholesterol: 120mg
Sodium: 420mg
Total carbohydrate: 24g
Dietary fiber: 3g
Sugars: 16g
Protein: 31g
Exchanges per serving
4 Meat, 3 Fat, 2 Vegetable, 1 Fruit

Citrus Glazed Chicken with Toasted Almonds

Prep time: 15 to 20 minutes
Bake time: 15 to 20 minutes

    4   boneless, skinless chicken breasts (total 1 pound)
    3   tablespoons orange juice concentrate, thawed
    2   tablespoons fresh lemon juice
   ½   cup chicken broth
    3   tablespoons SPLENDA® Granular
  1½   teaspoons cornstarch
    1   tablespoon unsalted butter
    1   tablespoon fresh chives, chopped
    1   tablespoon fresh parsley, stemmed and chopped
   ¼   cup sliced almonds, toasted

PREHEAT oven to 425°F. Place chicken breasts on foil-lined baking sheet. Brush with 1 tablespoon orange juice concentrate. Bake 15 to 20 minutes or until cooked through.

PLACE remaining orange juice concentrate, lemon juice and chicken broth in small saucepan. Blend SPLENDA® Granular and cornstarch in small bowl. Stir cornstarch mixture into broth. Heat over medium-high heat and simmer 8 to 10 minutes or until sauce thickens slightly. Remove from heat. Whisk butter into sauce. Add chives and parsley. Pour sauce over chicken breasts. Top with almonds.

SERVE with tossed salad or steamed vegetables.

Makes 4 servings
(1 piece chicken plus 3 tablespoons sauce)

Nutrients per serving Serving size: 1 piece chicken plus 3 tablespoons sauce	
Total calories:	230
Calories from fat:	70
Total fat:	7g
Saturated fat:	2.5g
Cholesterol:	75mg
Sodium:	190mg
Total carbohydrate:	9g
Dietary fiber:	1g
Sugars:	5g
Protein:	28g
Exchanges per serving ½ Starch, 4 Meat, 1 Fat	

Lemon Chicken

Chill time: *10 minutes*
Prep time: *10 to 15 minutes*

    2   teaspoons cornstarch, divided
    ¼   cup low-sodium soy sauce, divided
   12   ounces chicken breast tenders, cut in thirds
    ¼   cup fresh lemon juice
    ¼   cup fat-free chicken broth
    1   teaspoon fresh gingerroot, minced
    2   cloves garlic, peeled and minced
    2   teaspoons SPLENDA® Granular
    1   tablespoon vegetable oil
    ¼   cup red bell pepper, seeded and sliced
    ¼   cup green bell pepper, seeded and sliced

MIX 1 teaspoon cornstarch and 1 tablespoon soy sauce in medium bowl. Add sliced chicken tenders. Chill 10 minutes.

STIR lemon juice, remaining soy sauce, chicken broth, ginger, garlic, SPLENDA® Granular and 1 teaspoon cornstarch together in medium bowl to make sauce.

HEAT oil in medium frying pan. Add chicken and cook over medium-high heat for 3 to 4 minutes or until chicken is no longer pink in center. Add lemon sauce and sliced peppers. Cook 2 to 3 minutes more or until sauce thickens and peppers are hot.

SERVE with rice or Asian noodles.

Makes 4 servings
(3 ounces chicken, plus peppers and sauce)

Nutrients per serving
Serving size: 3 ounces chicken,
plus peppers and sauce
Total calories: 160
Calories from fat: 40
Total fat: 4.5g
Saturated fat: 0.5g
Cholesterol: 50mg
Sodium: 560mg
Total carbohydrate: 6g
Dietary fiber: 0g
Sugars: 2g
Protein: 22g
Exchanges per serving
3 Meat, 1 Vegetable, 1 Fat

Chili Meatloaf

Prep time: *15 minutes*
Bake time: *55 to 60 minutes*

1	cup tomato sauce, divided
3	tablespoons SPLENDA® Granular, divided
2	teaspoons prepared yellow mustard
1½	teaspoons chili powder, divided
1	tablespoon dried onion flakes
1	tablespoon dried parsley flakes
½	teaspoon salt
1	pound extra-lean ground turkey or beef
¼	cup Italian seasoned bread crumbs

PREHEAT oven to 350°F. Spray 9×5-inch loaf pan with nonstick cooking spray.

MIX ⅓ cup tomato sauce, 2 tablespoons SPLENDA® Granular, mustard, 1 teaspoon chili powder, onion flakes, parsley flakes and salt in large mixing bowl. Add ground meat and bread crumbs; stir well. Shape meat mixture into loaf form to fit pan; place in prepared pan.

MIX remaining tomato sauce, chili powder and SPLENDA® Granular together in small bowl. Spoon mixture over top of meatloaf.

BAKE 55 to 60 minutes. Remove meatloaf from oven and place on wire rack. Cool 5 minutes before slicing.

Makes 6 servings (5 ounces)

Nutrients per serving
Serving size: 5 ounces
Total calories: 120
Calories from fat: 70
Total fat: 5g
Saturated fat: 3g
Cholesterol: 30mg
Sodium: 580mg
Total carbohydrate: 8g
Dietary fiber: 1g
Sugars: 2g
Protein: 18g
Exchanges per serving
½ Starch, 2 Meat

Fresh & Fun

Sweet treats with SPLENDA® No Calorie Sweetener

Raspberry Ice Pops

Prep time: *20 minutes*
Freeze time: *6 hours or overnight*

- 4 cups frozen unsweetened raspberries, thawed
- ⅓ cup SPLENDA® Granular
- 1 tablespoon fresh lemon juice
- 1 tablespoon light corn syrup

PLACE all ingredients in blender or food processor. Blend until smooth. Strain mixture through sieve into small bowl, pressing firmly to extract as much liquid as possible. Discard seeds.

POUR extracted juice into ice pop molds and freeze at least 6 hours or overnight.

Makes 8 (¼-cup) frozen ice pops

Nutrients per serving Serving size: 1 ice pop	
Total calories: 35	Sodium: 0mg
Calories from fat: 0	Total carbohydrate: 9g
Total fat: 0g	Dietary fiber: 0g
Saturated fat: 0g	Sugars: 6g
Cholesterol: 0mg	Protein: 0g
	Exchanges per serving ½ **Fruit**

Candied Popcorn

Prep time: 15 minutes
Bake time: 20 to 25 minutes

13	cups freshly popped popcorn
1	egg white
2	tablespoons dark molasses
2	teaspoons vanilla extract
½	teaspoon salt
¾	cup SPLENDA® Granular
½	cup dry roasted peanuts

PREHEAT oven to 325°F. Spray an 11×13-inch pan with nonstick cooking spray and set aside.

PLACE popcorn in large bowl. In small bowl, add egg white, molasses, vanilla, salt and SPLENDA® Granular; whisk well. Add peanuts and stir until peanuts are coated. Pour over popcorn. Toss until popcorn is coated.

PLACE on prepared baking pan. Bake 20 to 25 minutes, stirring occasionally, until mix is crispy. Remove mix from oven and spread onto parchment or waxed paper to cool. Cool to room temperature before serving.

Makes 10 (1¼-cup) servings

Nutrients per serving
Serving size: 1¼ cups
Total calories: 110
Calories from fat: 35
Total fat: 4g
Saturated fat: 1g
Cholesterol: 0mg
Sodium: 240mg
Total carbohydrate: 15g
Dietary fiber: 2g
Sugars: 3g
Protein: 3g
Exchanges per serving
1 Starch, 1 Fat

Peanut Butter Chocolate Cheesecake Cups

Prep time: *25 minutes*
Bake time: *10 to 15 minutes*
Chill time: *2 hours*

Crust
36 low-fat chocolate wafer cookies
¼ cup SPLENDA® Granular
5 tablespoons light butter, melted

Peanut Butter Center
½ cup SPLENDA® Granular
3 tablespoons reduced-fat peanut butter
3 tablespoons low-fat cream cheese

Chocolate Filling
4 ounces unsweetened chocolate
8 ounces low-fat cream cheese
1¾ cups SPLENDA® Granular
½ cup skim milk
½ cup egg substitute
1 teaspoon vanilla extract
2 ounces sugar-free dark chocolate, melted (optional)

PREHEAT oven to 350°F.

CRUST: Crush cookies into fine crumbs. Blend all crust ingredients in small bowl. Set aside.

CENTER: Place all center ingredients in small bowl. Mix well and set aside.

FILLING: Melt chocolate in small saucepan over low heat. Set aside. Place cream cheese and SPLENDA® Granular in small mixing bowl. Beat until soft. Slowly add skim milk. Mix, using wire whisk, until smooth. Add melted chocolate and stir. Add egg substitute and vanilla and mix well.

ASSEMBLE: Place 24 mini-size foil baking cups on sheet pan. Divide crust evenly among 24 baking cups. Press crusts into bottom of cups. Place ½ teaspoon peanut butter mixture in center of each crust-lined baking cup. Spoon chocolate filling into each baking cup. Firmly tap sheet pan on countertop to remove air bubbles.

BAKE 10 to 15 minutes, or until slightly firm to touch. Chill 2 hours before serving. Drizzle melted chocolate over top of cups as garnish, if desired.

Makes 24 servings

Nutrients per serving
Serving size: 1 mini cup
Total calories: 130
Calories from fat: 60
Total fat: 8g
Saturated fat: 4g
Cholesterol: 10mg

Sodium: 150mg
Total carbohydrate: 12g
Dietary fiber: 1g
Sugars: 3g
Protein: 4g

Exchanges per serving
1 Starch, 1 Fat

Tempt Your
Sweet
Tooth

Cookies, bars, pudding and pies

Rice Pudding

Prep time: 10 minutes
Bake time: 55 to 65 minutes

½	cup egg substitute
2	cups nonfat milk
½	cup SPLENDA® Granular
½	cup raisins
1½	cups cooked white rice
1	teaspoon vanilla extract
½	teaspoon salt
1	teaspoon ground cinnamon
1	teaspoon ground nutmeg

Nutrients per serving	
Serving size: ¾ cup	
Total calories:	140
Calories from fat:	4
Total fat:	1g
Saturated fat:	0.5g
Cholesterol:	<5mg
Sodium:	300mg
Total carbohydrate:	30g
Dietary fiber:	1g
Sugars:	13g
Protein:	9g
Exchanges per serving	
1½ Starch, ½ Fat-Free Milk	

PREHEAT oven to 325°F. In large bowl, combine egg substitute, milk, SPLENDA® Granular, raisins, cooked rice, vanilla and salt. Mix well. Blend cinnamon and nutmeg in small bowl.

POUR rice mixture into 9×9-inch glass baking dish. Bake 25 minutes. Remove from oven. Sprinkle top with cinnamon mixture; return to oven and bake 40 minutes.

Makes 6 servings (¾ cup)

Lemon Raspberry Bars

Prep time: 10 minutes
Bake time: 35 to 45 minutes
Chill time: 2 hours

Crust:
- ¾ cup SPLENDA® Granular
- ¾ cup all-purpose flour
  Pinch salt
- ¼ cup light butter

Filling:
- 1¼ cups SPLENDA® Granular
- 2 tablespoons all-purpose flour
- ½ cup egg substitute
- ½ cup half-and-half
- ½ cup fresh lemon juice
- 1½ tablespoons grated fresh lemon peel
- ¼ cup fruit-only raspberry preserves

Nutrients per serving
Serving size: 1 bar
(2-inch square)
Total calories: 70
Calories from fat: 20
Total fat: 2.5g
Saturated fat: 1.5g
Cholesterol: 10mg
Sodium: 45mg
Total carbohydrate: 12g
Dietary fiber: 0g
Sugars: 3g
Protein: 2g
Exchanges per serving
1 Starch

PREHEAT oven to 350°F. Spray 8×8-inch baking pan with butter-flavor nonstick cooking spray.

MIX SPLENDA® Granular, flour and salt in medium bowl. Cut in light butter until mixture is crumbly. Do not overmix. Press dough into prepared baking pan. Bake 15 to 20 minutes or until lightly browned.

PLACE SPLENDA® Granular and flour in medium bowl. Stir well. Add egg substitute and half-and-half. Stir until blended. Slowly add lemon juice while stirring constantly; add lemon peel. In small bowl, stir raspberry preserves until liquified. Spread evenly over warm crust.

GENTLY pour lemon mixture over preserves. Bake 20 to 25 minutes or until set. Remove from oven and allow to cool before chilling. Chill in refrigerator 2 hours before serving.

Makes 16 (2-inch-square) bars

SPLENDA® and Spice Cookies

Prep time: 10 minutes
Chill time: 2 hours
Bake time: 10 to12 minutes

  6 tablespoons vegetable shortening
  6 tablespoons margarine
  1 cup SPLENDA® Granular
  1 egg
  ¼ cup molasses
  2 cups all-purpose flour, sifted
  ¾ teaspoon ground ginger
  1 teaspoon ground cinnamon
  ½ teaspoon ground cloves

MIX together shortening, margarine, SPLENDA® Granular, egg and molasses.

SIFT flour, ginger, cinnamon and cloves. Add to shortening mixture and stir to form dough. Wrap dough in plastic wrap. Chill dough in refrigerator until firm, about 2 hours.

PREHEAT oven to 350°F. Form dough into 30 balls (1 heaping teaspoon each). Place cookies on ungreased cookie sheet and pat down gently with fork, making criss-cross pattern.

BAKE cookies in center of oven for 10 to 12 minutes. Do not overbake. Cookies will look chewy but become crisp after cooling. Cool cookies on wire cooling rack.

Makes 30 cookies

Nutrients per serving
Serving size: 1 cookie
Total calories: 90
Calories from fat: 45
Total fat: 5g
Saturated fat: 1g
Cholesterol: 5mg
Sodium: 30mg
Total carbohydrate: 9g
Dietary fiber: 0g
Sugars: 2g
Protein: 1g
Exchanges per serving
½ Starch, 1 Fat

Cheery Cherry Pie

Prep time: *20 minutes (chill dough 30 minutes)*
Bake Time: *50 to 60 minutes*

Crust
- ¾ cup ice water
- 1 teaspoon vinegar (white or cider)
- 2 cups all-purpose flour, divided
- 3 tablespoons SPLENDA® Granular
- 7 tablespoons vegetable shortening

Filling
- 2 cans (14.5 ounces each) tart red cherries in water, drained, liquid reserved
- ¼ cup cornstarch
- ⅔ cup SPLENDA® Granular
- ¼ teaspoon almond extract
- 2 teaspoons fresh lemon juice
- 3 to 4 drops red food coloring (optional)

Crust:

MIX ice water and vinegar in cup. Place ½ cup flour in bowl, adding vinegar-water mix gradually, using wire whisk. Mix well. In separate bowl, combine remaining flour and SPLENDA® Granular. Add shortening, using pastry cutter or two knives until mixture is crumbly. Gradually add water-flour mixture, adding just enough to bind dough together.

DIVIDE dough in half. Gently pat each half into circle on floured work surface. Cover circles separately with plastic wrap and chill dough 30 minutes.

Filling:

DRAIN reserved canned cherry liquid through sieve into medium saucepan. Mix cornstarch and SPLENDA® Granular together in small bowl. Pour into saucepan. Stir well. Add almond extract

Nutrients per serving	
Serving size: 1 slice	
Total calories:	270
Calories from fat:	100
Total fat:	11g
Saturated fat:	2.5g
Cholesterol:	0mg
Sodium:	80mg
Total carbohydrate:	39g
Dietary fiber:	2g
Sugars:	8g
Protein:	4g
Exchanges per serving	
1½ Starch, 2 Fat, 1 Fruit	

and lemon juice. Stir and cook over medium heat. Simmer 3 to 4 minutes to thicken sauce. Remove from heat. If desired, add 3 to 4 drops of red food coloring and mix.

PLACE drained cherries in medium bowl. Pour liquid over cherries and gently fold with spatula to mix without crushing fruit. Set aside.

PREHEAT oven to 375°F. Spray 9-inch pie pan with nonstick cooking spray; set aside.

Assemble pie:

ROLL out 1 circle of dough on floured work surface to 11 inches in diameter. Place in prepared pie pan. Place filling in crust in pie pan. Roll remaining crust to 10 inches in diameter and place on top of filling. Crimp and seal edges with fingertips or fork. Use fork to prick top crust to allow steam to escape. Brush crust with milk for golden browning.

BAKE 50 to 60 minutes or until filling bubbles and crust is golden. Cool pie 1 hour before serving.

Makes 1 (9-inch) pie (8 servings)

Chocolate Chip Cookies

Prep time: *15 minutes*
Bake time: *10 to 12 minutes*

⅔ cup butter or margarine, softened
⅔ cup brown sugar, firmly packed
⅔ cup SPLENDA® Granular
2 teaspoons vanilla extract
2 eggs
1½ cups all-purpose flour
1 teaspoon baking soda
¼ teaspoon salt
1 cup semi-sweet chocolate chips

PREHEAT oven to 350°F.

BLEND butter, brown sugar, SPLENDA® Granular and vanilla in medium bowl. Stir until creamy.

ADD eggs, 1 at a time, mixing and scraping sides of bowl after each addition. Add flour, baking soda and salt; blend. Stir in chocolate chips.

PLACE level tablespoons of cookie dough on ungreased baking sheet. Bake 10 to 12 minutes or until golden brown. Remove from oven and cool on wire cooling rack.

Makes 36 cookies

Nutrients per serving
Serving size: 1 cookie
Total calories: 100
Calories from fat: 45
Total fat: 5g
Saturated fat: 3g
Cholesterol: 20mg
Sodium: 95mg
Total carbohydrate: 12g
Dietary fiber: 0g
Sugars: 6g
Protein: 1g
Exchanges per serving
1 Starch, 1 Fat

Easy Pear Crisp

Prep time: 15 minutes
Bake time: 40 to 50 minutes

½ cup SPLENDA® Granular, divided
3 graham crackers
¼ cup light butter
4 tablespoons all-purpose flour, divided
2 teaspoons ground cinnamon, divided
3 cups Bartlett pears, peeled, cored and sliced
1 tablespoon lemon juice
3 tablespoons water

PREHEAT oven to 350°F. Spray 8×8-inch baking dish with nonstick cooking spray.

PLACE ¼ cup SPLENDA® Granular, graham crackers, light butter, 2 tablespoons flour and 1 teaspoon cinnamon in bowl of food processor. Blend until crumbly.

TOSS remaining SPLENDA® Granular, flour, cinnamon, pears, lemon juice and water until fruit is evenly coated. Place in prepared baking pan. Cover with crumb topping.

BAKE 40 to 45 minutes or until bubbling around edges. Serve warm.

Makes 6 servings (2½-inch squares)

Nutrients per serving
Serving size: 1 (2½-inch) square
Total calories: 130
Calories from fat: 40
Total fat: 5g
Saturated fat: 2.5g
Cholesterol: 15mg
Sodium: 70mg
Total carbohydrate: 22g
Dietary fiber: 3g
Sugars: 9g
Protein: 2g

Exchanges per serving
½ Starch, 1 Fat, 1 Fruit

Apple Cranberry Pie

Prep time: 30 minutes (chill dough 30 minutes)
Bake time: 50 to 60 minutes

Crust
- ¾ cup ice water
- 1 teaspoon vinegar (white or cider)
- 2 cups all-purpose flour, divided
- 3 tablespoons SPLENDA® Granular
- 7 tablespoons vegetable shortening

Filling
- 1 cup fresh cranberries
- ½ cup SPLENDA® Granular
- 1 tablespoon all-purpose flour
- ½ teaspoon ground cinnamon
- 4 large Granny Smith apples, peeled, cored and sliced

Crust:

MIX ice water and vinegar in cup. Place ½ cup flour in bowl, adding vinegar-water mix gradually; whisk well. Combine remaining flour and SPLENDA® Granular in medium bowl. Add shortening, using pastry cutter or two knives, until mixture is crumbly. Gradually add water-flour mixture, adding just enough to bind dough together.

DIVIDE dough in half. Gently pat each half into circle on floured work surface. Cover circles separately with plastic wrap and chill dough 30 minutes.

Filling:

PREHEAT oven to 400°F. Coarsely chop cranberries. Mix all filling ingredients together in medium bowl. Spray 9-inch pie pan with nonstick cooking spray.

ROLL out 1 circle of dough on floured work surface to 11 inches in diameter. Place in prepared pie pan. Place filling in crust in pie pan. Roll remaining crust to 10 inches in diameter and place on top of filling. Crimp and seal edges with fingertips or fork. Use fork to prick top crust. Brush crust with milk for browning.

BAKE 50 to 60 minutes or until crust is golden.

Makes 1 (9-inch) pie (8 servings)

Nutrients per serving
Serving size: 1 slice

Total calories:	270
Calories from fat:	70
Total fat:	11g
Saturated fat:	3g
Cholesterol:	0mg
Sodium:	90mg
Total carbohydrate:	39g
Dietary fiber:	3g
Sugars:	10g
Protein:	4g

Exchanges per serving
1½ Starch, 2 Fat, 1 Fruit

Raspberry Heart Cookies

Prep time: *20 minutes*
Chill time: *1 hour*
Bake time: *8 to 10 minutes*

¾ cup unsalted butter, softened
¼ cup light butter, softened
1 cup SPLENDA® Granular
1 tablespoon vanilla extract
¼ cup egg substitute
¼ cup water
¾ teaspoon vinegar
  (white or cider)
1½ cups all-purpose flour
1½ cups cake flour
¼ teaspoon salt
1 teaspoon baking powder
⅓ cup sugar-free raspberry
  preserves
3 tablespoons "Powdered Sugar"
  (p. 88)

Nutrients per serving	
Serving size: 1 sandwich cookie	
Total calories:	170
Calories from fat:	90
Total fat:	10g
Saturated fat:	3.5g
Cholesterol:	25mg
Sodium:	85mg
Total carbohydrate:	19g
Dietary fiber:	0g
Sugars:	2g
Protein:	2g

Exchanges per serving
1 Starch, 2 Fat

BLEND together butters, SPLENDA® Granular and vanilla extract in medium bowl. Add egg substitute, water and vinegar; mix. Add flours, salt and baking powder. Mix with electric mixer on low speed (or by hand) until dough is formed. Scrape sides and bottom of bowl.

REMOVE dough from bowl and place on floured work surface. Divide dough in half and round each half into a 1-inch-thick flat disk. Wrap each dough portion in plastic wrap; chill 1 hour.

PREHEAT oven to 350°F. Oil 18×12-inch baking pan or cookie sheet.

UNWRAP dough and roll out on floured work surface to ⅛-inch thickness. Cut with large (3×4 inches) heart-shaped cookie cutters. Cut small heart shapes out of centers of half the cookies (these will top filled cookies). Place cookies on prepared pan.

BAKE 8 to 10 minutes or until lightly browned on bottom. Cool on wire rack.

SPRINKLE "Powdered Sugar" over top layer cookies (with center heart cut-outs). Spread 1 teaspoon raspberry preserves on remaining cookies. Place cookies with cut-outs on top of cookies spread with raspberry preserves.

Makes 18 sandwich cookies

Tempt Your Sweet Tooth | 67

Celebration
Cakes

Make celebrations special
with SPLENDA® No Calorie Sweetener

Low-Fat Lime Cheesecake

Prep time: *20 minutes*
Bake time: *50 to 60 minutes*
Chill time: *6 hours or overnight*

1	pound cream cheese
1	pound nonfat cream cheese
1¼	cups SPLENDA® Granular
2½	tablespoons fresh lime juice
2	tablespoons grated lime peel
	Pinch salt
4	eggs
1	Crust (recipe follows)

PREHEAT oven to 350°F.

BEAT cream cheeses and SPLENDA® Granular until smooth. Add fresh lime juice, grated peel and salt; beat until smooth. Add eggs, 1 at a time, scraping sides of bowl and beating well after each addition.

POUR cream cheese filling into prepared crust and bake 50 to 60 minutes or until slightly firm to touch. Remove from oven. Let cool 25 to 30 minutes before placing in refrigerator. Chill 6 hours or overnight before serving.

Makes 16 slices

Crust:

1¼	cup graham cracker crumbs
¼	cup SPLENDA® Granular
3	tablespoons butter, melted

MIX ingredients and press into 10-inch springform pan.

Makes 1 (10-inch) crust

Nutrients per serving
Serving size: 1 slice
Total calories: 210
Calories from fat: 130
Total fat: 14g
Saturated fat: 8g
Cholesterol: 95mg
Sodium: 340mg
Total carbohydrate: 10g
Dietary fiber: 0g
Sugars: 2g
Protein: 8g
Exchanges per serving
½ Starch, 1 Meat, 2 Fat

Yellow Cupcakes

Prep time: 20 minutes
Bake time: 12 to 15 minutes

2¼ cups cake flour
¾ cup SPLENDA® Granular
¼ cup granulated sugar
¾ cup unsalted butter, softened
½ cup nonfat instant dry milk
2 teaspoons baking powder
¾ teaspoon baking soda
¼ teaspoon salt
¾ cup buttermilk
3 eggs
2 teaspoons vanilla extract
½ teaspoon almond extract

Nutrients per serving Serving size: 1 cupcake without glaze	
Total calories:	160
Calories from fat:	80
Total fat:	9g
Saturated fat:	5g
Cholesterol:	60mg
Sodium:	170mg
Total carbohydrate:	16g
Dietary fiber:	0g
Sugars:	4g
Protein:	4g
Exchanges per serving **1 Starch, 2 Fat**	

PREHEAT oven to 350°F. Place 18 paper baking cups into muffin pans. Set aside.

PLACE cake flour, SPLENDA® Granular, sugar and softened butter in large bowl. Mix 1 to 2 minutes with electric mixer set on medium speed until butter is mixed into flour mixture.

ADD nonfat dry milk, baking powder, baking soda and salt. Mix on low speed until blended.

MIX buttermilk, eggs and extracts in small bowl. Stir well. Add ⅔ of buttermilk mixture to flour mixture. Mix on medium speed until just blended. Stop mixer and scrape sides and bottom of bowl. Mix on medium-high speed 45 to 60 seconds until batter appears lighter in color. Reduce mixer speed to low and add remaining buttermilk mixture. Mix on medium speed until blended. Stop mixer and scrape sides and bottom of bowl again. Mix on medium-high speed 30 seconds.

SPOON cake batter into prepared cups. Bake cupcakes 12 to 15 minutes or until wooden toothpick inserted in center of cupcake comes out clean. Top with **"Powdered Sugar" Glaze** (recipe on page 89).

Makes 18 cupcakes

Mocha Swirl Cheesecake

Prep time: 20 minutes
Bake time: 45 to 50 minutes
Chill time: 6 hours or overnight

1½ pounds low-fat cream cheese
¾ cup SPLENDA® Granular
2 eggs
2 egg whites
1½ tablespoons cornstarch
¼ teaspoon salt
¾ cup reduced-fat sour cream
2 teaspoons vanilla extract
1¼ teaspoons instant espresso
    crystals
2 packets (.55 ounces) sugar-
    free instant cocoa mix
1 Crust (recipe follows)

Nutrients per serving
Serving size: 1 slice
Total calories: 240
Calories from fat: 120
Total fat: 14g
Saturated fat: 8g
Cholesterol: 60mg
Sodium: 400mg
Total carbohydrate: 19g
Dietary fiber: 0g
Sugars: 10g
Protein: 7g
Exchanges per serving
1½ Starch, ½ Meat, 3 Fat

PREHEAT oven to 325°F. Beat cream cheese and SPLENDA®
Granular together until smooth. Add eggs, egg whites, cornstarch and
salt. Mix until smooth, scraping sides of bowl. Add sour cream and
vanilla and blend.

MEASURE ½ cup of cheesecake batter and pour into small bowl. Add
instant espresso crystals and cocoa mix. Stir until dissolved.

POUR half of plain batter over crust. Divide mocha mixture and
place spoonfuls of ½ mocha mixture over plain batter. Gently swirl
into plain batter with tip of knife or spatula. Repeat layers and swirls
with remaining batters.

BAKE 45 to 50 minutes or until center is almost set. Remove from
oven and gently run metal spatula around rim of pan to loosen
cheesecake (this helps prevent cracking). Let cool 60 minutes before
covering and placing in refrigerator. Chill 6 hours or overnight before
serving.

Crust:
44 low-fat chocolate wafers, crushed
¼ cup butter, melted
2 tablespoons unsweetened cocoa powder
¼ cup SPLENDA® Granular

PREHEAT oven to 400°F. Mix crust ingredients together and press into 9-inch springform pan. Place pan on baking sheet and bake 10 minutes. Remove from oven and cool to room temperature.

Makes 1 (10-inch) cheesecake (16 slices)

Dulce de Leche Cheesecake

Prep time: 20 minutes
Bake time: 45 to 55 minutes
Chill time: 6 hours or overnight

1½ pounds low-fat cream cheese
1 cup SPLENDA® Granular
2 tablespoons all-purpose flour
2 teaspoons vanilla extract
3 eggs
⅓ cup low-fat milk
½ cup dulce de leche*
1 Crust (recipe follows)

(caramelized milk topping sold in Hispanic food sections at most supermarkets)

PREHEAT oven to 325°F.

BEAT cream cheese, SPLENDA® Granular and flour together until well mixed and smooth. Add vanilla and mix until blended. Add eggs, 1 at a time, scraping sides of bowl and beating well after each addition. Mix until smooth. Add milk and blend.

MEASURE ½ cup of cheesecake batter and pour into small bowl. Add dulce de leche and stir until well combined.

POUR plain batter over crust. Place spoonfuls of dulce de leche batter over plain batter. Gently swirl into plain batter with tip of knife or spatula.

BAKE 45 to 55 minutes or until center is almost set. Remove from oven and gently run metal spatula around rim of pan to loosen cheesecake (this helps prevent cracking). Cool 20 to 25 minutes before covering and placing in refrigerator. Chill 6 hours or overnight before serving.

Makes 1 (10-inch) cheesecake
(16 slices)

Crust:
1 cup graham cracker crumbs
3 tablespoons butter, melted

PREHEAT oven to 400°F. Mix crust ingredients together, and press into 9-inch springform pan. Place pan on baking sheet and bake 8 to 10 minutes. Remove from oven and cool.

Makes 1 (9-inch) crust

Nutrients per serving	
Serving size: 1 slice	
Total calories:	190
Calories from fat:	110
Total fat:	12g
Saturated fat:	7g
Cholesterol:	70mg
Sodium:	200mg
Total carbohydrate:	15g
Dietary fiber:	0g
Sugars:	9g
Protein:	7g
Exchanges per serving	
1 Starch, 1 Meat, 1 Fat	

Delightful
Drinks

Guilt-free sips with SPLENDA® No Calorie Sweetener

Strawberry-Orange Smash

Prep time: 5 minutes

2½ cups frozen, unsweetened strawberries
½ cup SPLENDA® Granular
1 cup calcium-fortified orange juice
¾ cup nonfat plain yogurt
½ teaspoon vanilla extract
¼ cup ice cubes

PLACE all ingredients in blender. Mix on low speed 15 to 20 seconds. Remove lid. Stir well. Cover and blend on medium speed until smooth.

POUR into 4 glasses and serve immediately.

Makes 4 (8-ounce) servings

Nutrients per serving Serving size: 8 ounces	
Total calories: 100	Sodium: 40mg
Calories from fat: 0	Total carbohydrate: 21g
Total fat: 0g	Dietary fiber: 2g
Saturated fat: 0g	Sugars: 14g
Cholesterol: 0mg	Protein: 4g
	Exchanges per serving 1½ Fruit

Hot Chocolate

Prep time: 10 minutes

- 2 cups reduced-fat milk
- 8 packets SPLENDA® No Calorie Sweetener
- 3 tablespoons powdered cocoa
  (preferably Dutch processed)

Garnish:
- 2 tablespoons reduced-calorie
  whipped topping
- ¼ teaspoon ground cinnamon

PLACE milk in small saucepan. Mix contents of SPLENDA® Packets and cocoa powder in small bowl. Add to milk and whisk well. Simmer 4 to 5 minutes over medium-low heat until steaming.

POUR mixture into 2 serving cups. Optional garnish: Top each with 1 tablespoon reduced-calorie whipped topping and pinch of ground cinnamon.

Makes 2 (8 fluid ounces) servings

Nutrients per serving
Serving size: 8 fluid ounces
Total calories: 160
Calories from fat: 50
Total fat: 6g
Saturated fat: 3.5g
Cholesterol: 20mg
Sodium: 130mg
Total carbohydrate: 20g
Dietary fiber: 3g
Sugars: 12g
Protein: 10g
Exchanges per serving
½ Starch, 1 Reduced-Fat Milk

Banana Raspberry Smoothie

Prep time: 15 minutes

- 1 large ripe banana, sliced
- 5 packets SPLENDA® No Calorie Sweetener
- ½ cup nonfat milk
- 1¼ cups frozen unsweetened raspberries

PLACE sliced banana on plate and freeze for 10 minutes or until slightly firm.

COMBINE all ingredients in blender. Blend on medium speed until smooth. Pour into 2 glasses and serve immediately.

Makes 2 (8 fluid ounces) servings

Nutrients per serving
Serving size: 8 fluid ounces
Total calories: 110
Calories from fat: 0
Total fat: 0g
Saturated fat: 0g
Cholesterol: 0mg
Sodium: 30mg
Total carbohydrate: 25g
Dietary fiber: 4g
Sugars: 19g
Protein: 3g
Exchanges per serving
1½ Fruit

Elegant Eggnog

Prep time: 20 minutes
Chill time: 5 hours or overnight

1	cup SPLENDA® Granular
1	tablespoon arrowroot powder or cornstarch
1	teaspoon ground nutmeg
7	egg yolks
4	cups whole milk
2	cups nonfat half-and-half
2	tablespoons vanilla extract

MIX SPLENDA® Granular, arrowroot powder and nutmeg in large bowl. In separate bowl, whisk egg yolks until smooth. Add egg yolks to SPLENDA® Granular mixture and whisk.

ADD milk slowly while stirring continuously.

POUR mixture into large, heavy saucepan and place over low heat. Whisk while heating.

CONTINUE whisking until temperature reaches 175°F,* about 5 to 8 minutes.

REMOVE from heat and blend in half-and-half.

POUR eggnog into food-safe container and chill approximately 2 hours uncovered. Cover eggnog after 2 hours and chill at least 3 hours more before serving. Add vanilla extract just before serving. Eggnog will keep 3 days in refrigerator.

Makes 14 to 16 (½-cup) servings

*Be sure to cook to 175°F as this temperature kills any bacteria in the egg yolks. You may add 1 teaspoon dark rum per serving for an adult; however, nutrient data will change.

Nutrients per serving
Serving size: ½ cup plain

Total calories: 100
Calories from fat: 45
Total fat: 5g
Saturated fat: 2g
Cholesterol: 120mg
Sodium: 70mg
Total carbohydrate: 9g
Dietary fiber: 0g
Sugars: 6g
Protein: 5g

Exchanges per serving
½ Starch, 2 Fat

Lemonade

Prep time: 5 minutes

- 2 slices lemon
- 2 teaspoons lemon juice
- 3 packets SPLENDA® No Calorie Sweetener
- ½ cup club soda
- ¾ cup ice cubes
  Fresh mint leaves, washed

MASH lemon slices, lemon juice and contents of SPLENDA® Packets with fork or spoon in tall glass. Add club soda and ice cubes; garnish with mint leaves and serve.

Makes 1 (8 fluid ounces) serving

Nutrients per serving
Serving size: 8 fluid ounces
Total calories: 20
Calories from fat: 0
Total fat: 0g
Saturated fat: 0g
Cholesterol: 0mg
Sodium: 25mg
Total carbohydrate: 5g
Dietary fiber: 0g
Sugars: 2g
Protein: 0g
Exchanges per serving
Free

Mulled Cider

Prep time: 5 minutes
Cook time: 30 to 60 minutes

- 8 cups unsweetened apple cider
- ½ cup SPLENDA® Granular
- 16 whole cloves
- 6 whole allspice
- 5 whole cinnamon sticks
- ½ cup dried unsweetened cranberries
- ⅓ cup fresh lemon juice
- 8 oranges, thinly sliced
- 8 lemons, thinly sliced

PLACE cider, SPLENDA® Granular, spices, cranberries and lemon juice in medium pot. Heat over medium-low heat 30 to 60 minutes. Do not boil.

ADD fruit slices 10 minutes before serving. As a precaution, strain cider to remove solids before serving to children. Serve warm.

Makes 16 (4 fluid ounces) servings

Nutrients per serving
Serving size: 4 fluid ounces
Total calories: 80
Calories from fat: 0
Total fat: 0g
Saturated fat: 0g
Cholesterol: 0mg
Sodium: 5mg
Total carbohydrate: 19g
Dietary fiber: 0g
Sugars: 16g
Protein: 0g
Exchanges per serving
1 Fruit

 **Staples**

Sweet substitutes to make better meals

Cranberry-Apple Relish

Prep time: 5 minutes
Cook time: 10 to 15 minutes

1 bag (12 ounces) fresh
   cranberries
1 cup SPLENDA® Granular
1 cup water
3 tablespoons orange juice
   concentrate
1 medium apple, peeled,
   cored and diced
⅓ cup golden raisins

PLACE cranberries, SPLENDA®
Granular, water and orange juice
concentrate in medium saucepan.
Bring to boil; boil 3 to 4 minutes
or until cranberries start to
thicken and water has reduced
by about half.

POUR into bowl. Cover and
chill 2 to 3 hours or overnight.

ADD diced apple and ½ of raisins
to cranberries. Stir well.

CHILL until ready to serve. Just
before serving, sprinkle remaining
raisins over cranberries as garnish.
Serve chilled with roast meats or
poultry.

Makes 20 (1-ounce) servings

Nutrients per serving
Serving size: 1 ounce
Total calories: 30
Calories from fat: 0
Total fat: 0g
Saturated fat: 0g
Cholesterol: 0mg
Sodium: 0mg
Total carbohydrate: 7g
Dietary fiber: 1g
Sugars: 4g
Protein: 0g
Exchanges per serving
½ Fruit

"Powdered Sugar"

Prep time: *5 minutes*

¾ cup SPLENDA® Granular
2 tablespoons cornstarch

PLACE ingredients in blender. Cover and blend until SPLENDA® Granular is ground into a very fine powder. Use instead of powdered sugar to garnish cakes and pastries.

Makes ½ cup

Nutrients per serving
Serving size: 1 tablespoon
Total calories: 15
Calories from fat: 0
Total fat: 0g
Saturated fat: 0g
Cholesterol: 0mg
Sodium: 0mg
Total carbohydrate: 4g
Dietary fiber: 0g
Sugars: 0g
Protein: 0g
Exchanges per serving
Free

"Brown Sugar"

Prep time: *2 to 3 minutes*

1 cup SPLENDA® Granular
¼ cup sugar-free maple syrup

POUR ingredients into small mixing bowl and mix well. Use instead of brown sugar in recipes for baked goods.

Makes ¼ cup*

*This makes enough to replace 1 cup of standard brown sugar. It is best used as an ingredient, not as a topping or eaten plain.

Nutrients per serving
Serving size: 6 ounces
Total calories: 90
Calories from fat: 0
Total fat: 0g
Saturated fat: 0g
Cholesterol: 0mg
Sodium: 30mg
Total carbohydrate: 24g
Dietary fiber: 0g
Sugars: 0g
Protein: 0g
Exchanges per serving
1½ Fruit

"Powdered Sugar" Glaze

Prep time: *10 minutes*

1½ cups SPLENDA® Granular
¼   cup cornstarch
5   to 6 teaspoons water

PLACE SPLENDA® Granular and cornstarch in blender. Cover and blend until SPLENDA® Granular is finely powdered. Pour into small bowl. Add water and stir well.

NOTE: This recipe makes a thick glaze. Add more water for a thinner glaze.

VARIATIONS: Add:
½ teaspoon vanilla extract, or
1 drop maple flavor, or
1 teaspoon grated lemon peel or
1 teaspoon grated orange peel.

Makes ⅓ cup

Nutrients per serving
Serving size: 1 tablespoon
Total calories: 50
Calories from fat: 0
Total fat: 0g
Saturated fat: 0g
Cholesterol: 0mg
Sodium: 5mg
Total carbohydrate: 12g
Dietary fiber: 0g
Sugars: 0g
Protein: 0g
Exchanges per serving
1 Fruit

Low-Fat Cream Cheese Frosting

Prep time: *10 minutes*

½ cup light butter, softened
1   cup SPLENDA® Granular
1   pound nonfat cream
     cheese, softened
2   teaspoons vanilla extract

BEAT softened butter and SPLENDA® Granular briefly in medium bowl until SPLENDA® is just incorporated. Add cream cheese, tablespoon by tablespoon. Mix until lump free, 1 to 2 minutes. Scrape sides of bowl and add vanilla extract. Mix well.

Makes about 2 cups

Nutrients per serving
Serving size: 2 tablespoons
Total calories: 60
Calories from fat: 30
Total fat: 3g
Saturated fat: 2g
Cholesterol: 10mg
Sodium: 190mg
Total carbohydrate: 3g
Dietary fiber: 0g
Sugars: 0g
Protein: 3g
Exchanges per serving
1 Fat

BBQ Sauce

Prep time: *45 minutes*

 1 tablespoon canola or extra virgin olive oil
 1 cup onion, peeled and minced
 2 garlic cloves, peeled and minced
 2 low-sodium beef bouillon cubes
 ½ cup hot water
 3 cans (6 ounces each) tomato paste
 1 cup SPLENDA® Granular
 ¾ cup Worcestershire sauce
 ¾ cup Dijon mustard
 3 tablespoons hickory-flavored liquid smoke
 1 teaspoon salt
 ½ cup cider vinegar
 1 tablespoon hot pepper sauce or to taste

PLACE oil in large saucepan. Add onions and garlic. Sauté over medium heat until translucent, 2 to 3 minutes.

MIX bouillon and water. Add bouillon mixture and all remaining ingredients to saucepan. Stir well using wire whisk.

SIMMER uncovered 25 to 30 minutes; stir often. Chill overnight in nonreactive container to allow flavors to meld. Sauce is best if prepared 1 day before use. Keeps for 1 week, covered in refrigerator.

Makes about 6 cups

Nutrients per serving
Serving size: 2 tablespoons
Total calories: 20
Calories from fat: 0
Total fat: 0g
Saturated fat: 0g
Cholesterol: 0mg
Sodium: 240mg
Total carbohydrate: 4g
Dietary fiber: 0g
Sugars: 1g
Protein: 0g
Exchanges per serving
Free

Italian Dressing

Prep time: 2 to 3 minutes

½ cup canola or olive oil
¼ cup white wine vinegar
2 teaspoons dried basil
1½ teaspoons salt
1 teaspoon SPLENDA®
   No Calorie Sweetener
½ teaspoon garlic powder
1 tablespoon low-fat
   mayonnaise
3 tablespoons water

COMBINE all ingredients in blender. Blend on high until combined, approximately 30 seconds. Pour into small pitcher or salad dressing bottle. Cover and chill until ready to serve. Shake or stir before serving.

Makes about 1 cup

Nutrients per serving
Serving size: 2 tablespoons
Total calories: 120
Calories from fat: 100
Total fat: 14g
Saturated fat: 1g
Cholesterol: 0mg
Sodium: 450mg
Total carbohydrate: 1g
Dietary fiber: 0g
Sugars: 0g
Protein: 0g
Exchanges per serving
3 Fat

Spicy Peanut Sauce

Prep time: 5 minutes

½ cup chunky or smooth
   peanut butter
2 garlic cloves, quartered
1 tablespoon coarsely
   chopped fresh ginger
1 small fresh hot pepper,
   cleaned and diced
¼ cup peanut oil
2 tablespoons soy sauce
2 tablespoons SPLENDA®
   Granular
2 tablespoons rice vinegar
1 tablespoon sesame oil
¼ cup strong tea

PLACE all ingredients in food processor; purée to make sauce. Serve with chicken or noodle salad.

Makes about 1½ cups

Nutrients per serving
Serving size: 2 tablespoons
Total calories: 120
Calories from fat: 90
Total fat: 11g
Saturated fat: 2g
Cholesterol: 0mg
Sodium: 220mg
Total carbohydrate: 3g
Dietary fiber: 1g
Sugars: 1g
Protein: 3g
Exchanges per serving
½ Starch, 2 Fat

Index

60